21 DAYS WITH GOD

A Fasting and Prayer Guide for New Beginnings

SEYI HOPEWELL

21 DAYS WITH GOD
A Fasting and Prayer Guide for New Beginnings

Copyright © 2018 by Seyi Hopewell

ISBN: 978-1-944652-52-4

Printed in the United States of America. All rights reserved solely by the publisher. This book or parts thereof may not be reproduced in any form, stored in a retrieval system, or transmitted in any form by any means - electronic, mechanical, photocopy. Unless otherwise noted, Bible quotations are taken from the Holy Bible, New King James Version. Copyright 1982 by Thomas Nelson, Inc., publishers. Used by permission. Other scriptures are taking from Message (MSG) and New Living Translation (NLT).

Cornerstone Publishing
A Division of Cornerstone Creativity Group LLC
Phone: +1(516) 547-4999
info@thecornerstonepublishers.com
www.thecornerstonepublishers.com

To order bulk copies of this book or to contact the author please call 832-909-9787 or
email: thetruelightministry17@gmail.com

DEDICATION

This book is hereby dedicated to you; yes to the one who has decided to fast and pray in this New Year expecting new beginnings!

I will be using this book yearly as a birthday exercise and I pray that as you prayerfully use this book along with me while fasting; living a devout Christian life and abstaining from all appearances of sin, you will receive speedy answers to your prayers for a new beginning also in Jesus Name!

ACKNOWLEDGMENTS

I cannot begin this book without first acknowledging the Ocean Divider, Protocol Breaker and my Heavenly Father; our Savior Jesus Christ and our sweet Holy Spirit. I thank God for the divine inspiration about 21 days received in July 2017 and the leading of the Holy Spirit to write this book.

I wish to thank from the bottom of my heart, my family for their support and love. I thank the 5K5 Midnight Crew, my Church family Destinystar International Ministries and my Pastors worldwide for praying for me always to fulfill my calling.

For I know the plans I have for you," says the Lord. "They are plans for good and not for disaster, to give you a future and a hope. In those days when you pray, I will listen. (Jeremiah 29:11).

CONTENTS

Dedication..5
Acknowledgments....................................6

1. I have Perfect Peace...........................8
2. Fight against Fear.............................12
3. Joy in my heart.................................16
4. Go and Sin NO MORE....................20
5. Heal Me!...24
6. Build Me Up (I)................................28
7. Build Me Up (II)...............................32
8. Deliver Me..36
9. Confusion Cancelled........................40
10. Locked up but not Locked out.........44
11. Miracle Money.................................48
12. Increase my Faith.............................52
13. The Holy Spirit................................56
14. I shall Overcome..............................60
15. I shall not be Lukewarm...................64

16. I Forgive!..68
17. I can do ALL things!...................72
18. I will not worry!............................76
19. I MUST Endure..........................80
20. Speak LIFE.................................84
21. Prophesy over your life!............90

Testimonies After Trials..................96
Are You Saved?..............................110

Day 1
I HAVE PERFECT PEACE

You will keep in perfect peace all who trust in you, all whose thoughts are fixed on you!
—Isaiah 26:3

When I found this scripture and began to pray it over my life, I found it helpful to confess it often to help maintain peace in my life. Many times during this fast-paced life we live, it helps to confess it; especially when our minds are restless about a situation we are faced with such as paying bills, changing jobs, relocating, praying about marriage, nursing children or providing for the family.

As a woman in Ministry, I have learned to keep this scripture memorized because it is quite easy to fear or worry when life throws an unexpected curve ball. Rather than take on distress because of what you are passing through; it helps a great deal to confess loudly in declaration so that the demons of depression can hear you say, "Lord, You keep me in perfect peace because I trust in you and my mind is fixed on you!" Supernaturally, what you are passing through will lead you to a breakthrough in Jesus mighty name.

PRAYER POINTS

1. Father in Jesus Name, I thank you for this word; I CHOOSE to trust in you because you keep in perfect peace those who trust in you and those whose thoughts are FIXED on you!

2. As I commit this day of fasting to you Oh God, I surrender my mind, body, soul and spirit unto you. Empower me Lord with your peace, empower me with WISDOM to fix my mind on you and the word of God in Jesus Name!

3. Lord when situations arise and wicked people arise to disturb my peace, FIX my mind Lord!

4. Lord I know that times are tough for many but with your peace, I boldly declare that all my needs are met in Jesus Name because

you are Jehovah Jireh, MY provider!

5. And he arose, and rebuked the wind, and said unto the sea, Peace, be still. And the wind ceased, and there was a great calm. Mark 4:39 KJV

6. Jesus, while you were asleep, there was a storm which caused great fear in your disciples and they woke you up in a panic. Lord, I am also in fear (truthfully) about_____ so I'm waking you up now Lord. Wake up in me Jesus. Wake up in Me now Lord!

7. Just as Jesus did, I also arise (without fear) and I rebuke every contrary wind in my life. I speak to all winds in my marriage, in my finances, in my career, my business, my health and in the life of my children – I say unto you all – PEACE, BE STILL in Jesus Name!

And the peace of God, which passeth all understanding, shall keep your hearts and minds through Christ Jesus. (Phillipians 4:7 KJV)

Feeling better already aren't you?

Use this page to document and rejoice about the stillness of that storm you prayed about. Name the storm and when the testimony abounds, fill up this page!

Example: I need_____
_____I am believing God for this and I will be at peace until I get it in Jesus Name.

When your breakthrough manifests, come back here to document how the Lord did it! Example: The creditor reduced my debt and simultaneously, I had an unexpected check come in for the exact amount I needed so I paid it off! Praise God!

Day 2
FIGHT AGAINST FEAR

For God hath not given us the spirit of fear; but of power, and of love, and of a sound mind
— 2 Timothy 1:7

No one can say that they have never had fear! We all find ways to overcome fear but no one can tell me that they have never had a reason to fear. One night after a prayer revival, I was driving some pastors back to their hotel and in our jubilation of a mighty testimony that had occurred, I did not realize that I was speeding past a police officer. I was immediately pulled over and questioned and in that moment, fear gripped me because I did not want another ticket. I had other parking tickets that I had just paid for hence my fear of another one. I suddenly began to speak to the fear and I did so by confessing this:

Father, you did not give me the spirit of fear but of power and of love and of a sound mind so therefore by your power, touch the heart of this cop and let love change his mind and give me just a warning! He came back five minutes later, asked where we were coming from, we all said "church!!" and to our surprise he said "Praise God!" we all said Halleluyah and he gave me a warning and asked me to drive carefully!

Jesus asked his disciples in Mark 4:40 "why are you so afraid?" and he calmed the storm. Therefore I ask, that everything I have been so afraid of meet with Jesus today and obey His voice – I am not afraid, for Jesus is on the boat of this situation!

PRAYER POINTS
1. Father in Jesus name, I speak to every fearful situation in my life and invoke the overcoming power of Jesus to keep me standing tall and mighty.

2. Every sickness, disease, lack, bankruptcy, repossession, attack, court hearing, judgement, foreclosure, negative balance, loss, etc that is

causing fear in my life, I pull you down with the power in the name of Jesus Christ.

3. I will not be afraid. Like young David, I too will stand and fight against every Goliath of fear in my life and I shall be victorious in Jesus Name.

4. Oh Lord, make me laugh last in Jesus Name. I release the baggage fear and embrace power, the love of God and sound mind now in Jesus Name.

5. As I continue in this fast, Lord increase my faith through signs, revelations, dreams and great things that will happen for me and my family in Jesus Name.

Day 3
JOY IN MY HEART

Testimony

Lord I thank You for what You have done in my life. Sometimes as humans we find it hard to let go of something that we ourselves know is not making us happy but Lord in Your powerful way, You bring to pass that which You know I really needed. For men will lift you up today and bring you down tomorrow but God You remain the same forever. Thank You Lord for manifesting Yourself in my life and giving me this unspeakable joy in my heart.

—Mary May

When we have been through some things, it helps to have a grateful heart and this in turn will eventually give us joy in our hearts. Through good times and bad time, let us have joy in our hearts.

PRAYER POINTS

1. Father in the name of Jesus, it is you who

gives me joy down deep in my soul, so I have come to say thank you. On behalf of all my family, friends and loved ones, I say thank you Lord.

2. Thank you for all that you have done in my life. (Count your blessings, name them one by one and it will surprise you what the Lord has done).

3. Lord, in the name of Jesus, every situation that has affected the joy in my heart for so long; today, by your power, I bring them to your feet and drop it completely.

4. I give my heart to you Lord just like David did and ask that you fill it with joy in Jesus Mighty Name. I decree that I will be filled with joy because of you in Jesus Name.

5. Powers zapping joy from my life, according to the word of God in Psalm 9:16 – The Lord is known for justice and the wicked have trapped themselves in their own snare. I command you powers of darkness to trap yourselves in your own snare in Jesus name!

6. I receive the full joy of the Lord in my heart because I know that the joy of the Lord is my strength. Therefore I welcome your strength, peace, joy, success, good news, good reports, approvals, justice, breakthrough and all other good and perfect things in Jesus Name.

Day 4
GO AND SIN NO MORE

Listen! The Lord's arm is not too weak to save you, nor is his ear too deaf to hear you call. It's your sins that have cut you off from God. Because of your sins, he has turned away and will not listen anymore. Your hands are the hands of murderers, and your fingers are filthy with sin. Your lips are full of lies, and your mouth spews corruption.

—Isaiah 59: 1-3

When we choose to turn a deaf ear to the sovereign word of God, He can also turn his ear away. Our prayers are that this will never happen but effect of SIN is the very reason why King Saul had to go to a medium to call up the spirit of Prophet Samuel. He desperately needed to hear from God but God had turned his ear from Saul because he was disobedient and full of hatred (sin). What are you doing that can cause God to turn his ear? Our prayers are going to target the areas of sin in our life and by God's grace, we shall be restored to a place of righteousness in Him. In Luke 7, Jesus was anointed by a sinful woman who recognized herself as a sinner and she did the most beautiful thing by washing the feet of our Master with her tears and wiping them with her hair. She kissed his feet; anointing them with expensive perfume and the Bible recorded that Jesus defended her because of her act of repentance telling her directly "Your sins are forgiven." However when we choose to keep living in sin, how can we find His forgiveness?

PRAYER POINTS

1. Father I have sinned against you. I come to you now to confess my sins before you (name them) and I ask you for forgiveness now in Jesus Name.

2. According to your word - please Lord, soak me in your laundry and I shall come out clean, scrub me of my sins and I shall come out whiter than snow – Psalm 51:7 MSG Pray earnestly and repent of ALL sins and REPENT of your sins – never return to your vomit.

3. Father in the name of Jesus, according

to your work in Isaiah 57:15 I receive the refreshment you give to the humble and the new courage you give to those with repentant hearts. (Receive the courage to walk with your head up now)

4. When the teachers of religious law and the Pharisees brought a woman they had caught in the act of adultery before Jesus and told Him that the Law of Moses says to STONE HER! They had a pre-determined plan for her, so Jesus said "Alright, stone her." "But let those who have never sinned throw the first stones!" Everyone left her alone. Father, even the world condemns me, as long as it is you and I left standing, I receive your love.

5. Father I repent of all my sins today ask for mercy like you showed the woman caught in the act of adultery – Jesus son of David, have mercy on me.

6. Because you did not condemn me Oh my God, I will go and sin no more in Jesus Name!

Day 5
HEAL ME!

Suddenly, a man with leprosy approached him and knelt before him. "Lord," the man said, "if you are willing, you can heal me and make me clean." Jesus reached out and touched him. "I am willing," he said. "Be healed!" And instantly the leprosy disappeared.
—Matthew 8:2-3

Testimony

I've been smoking for 25 years and last week, I started having terrible chest pain, and I felt that my windpipe was blocking and so I was getting short of breath. But on day 45 of the firepower prayers when you were praying and you mentioned that we should touch anywhere we want God to heal us. That morning, I never believed I'll live to see the next day. But you started speaking in tongues, I started sweating and shaking, I began to feel a soothing touch in my chest. I got an instant healing. And today, that suicidal urge to smoke is gone forever. I give God all the glory and thank you so much ma. God bless you real good. May your fire never die in Jesus mighty name. (Amen)

Noah G.

1. Father I thank you because you are Jehovah Rapha our healer. Thank you for the times when you have healed me and my spouse and/or children.

2. Lord Jesus I come to you now for healing of my mind, my body and my spirit, if you are willing you can heal me and make me clean.

3. Any powers, any tragedy fashioned against my mental, physical, emotional and spiritual being backfire now in Jesus Name.

4. Father in Jesus Name, you said that you are willing to heal so I receive an instant healing just like the man with leprosy and I command permanent healing from today in Jesus Name.

5. As you healed many people during midnight prayers because of their faith,

Lord I connect with the miracles that occurred on that broadcast and place my hands wherever healing is needed…
….I RECEIVE MY HEALING FROM _____ IN THE MIGHTY NAME OF JESUS!

6. I lay my hands on all my documents, my accounts, my money, my home, my children and command the supernatural healing of God to begin to flow now in Jesus Name

7. As the Prophet of my own life, I prophesy healing, breakthrough and deliverance upon my destiny and the destiny of my children and spouse

8. I decree healing over the land of America and every nation represented.

More Testimonies of Healing:
Woman of God asked us to place our hands where it was hurting one night on the broadcast and immediately she prayed, the pain disappeared. I have not used any medicine since then! Praise God

—Sis Nora

I slept like a baby the night that Sis Seyi slept in our home in Minnesota. I invited her for the Domestic Violence Awareness and I cannot believe she came and stayed in our home. I have been walking with a limp for months now since my ordeal with my wicked husband but that night, on the midnight broadcast she prayed for me and anointed me with oil it was dripping all over my face. The morning after the prayer, I was running up and down the stairs. I have not limped since that day or felt any pain. God is real. He is a healer and I am a firm believer!

—Christine Dennis

Day 6:
BUILD ME UP (I)

I am forgotten like a dead man, out of mind; I am like a broken vessel.

—Psalm 31:12

People want to build their bodies and build businesses but only broken vessels can be built. David was one of the most broken vessels that the Bible recorded and this was why He was deemed "a man after God's heart." God is looking for broken vessels not puffy vessels. Which are you? Are you broken in your ways or are you "all that and a bag of chips?"

1. Father I thank you for your love for me and my family. All I have is by you and from you to glorify you O God!

2. In the name of Jesus, I humble myself and seek forgiveness for building myself

up before the mirror, before people, and before everyone else but you.

3. Father forgive me. I repent of pride because according to Proverbs 16:18 pride goes before destruction, and haughtiness before a fall. Build me up Lord for your sake in Jesus Name!

4. Any wicked power tearing me down as I build myself up in your word, your knowledge, your wisdom and your grace, be destroyed in Jesus Name!

5. But you, dear friends, must build each other up in your most holy faith, pray in the power of the Holy Spirit – Jude 1:20. In the name of Jesus, I receive the grace of God to study my Bible and I receive the infilling of the Holy Spirit now by fire.

6. Everything distracting my focus, causing me to sin, causing me back slide and neglect the building of my inner man, I rebuke you in Jesus Name.

7. Witchcraft agendas against my life to tear

me down, I come against you by the blood of Jesus Christ, be destroyed and disappear in Jesus name I pray. Amen

8. Prophesy over your life that you will stay in the way of building and you will not stop building your inner man for strength in God.

Day 7
BUILD ME UP (II)

God is able to do all things. I have learned to trust him more and more. The enemy will not succeed. I have overcome and they will see the glory of God manifest in me. Luke 10:19 tells me that my God have given me authority to trample on snakes and scorpions and to overcome all the power of the enemy nothing will harm me. Thanks to you also for your teaching I can now read my Bible and pray using scriptures. God is good and He's able!
—Christine Dennis

Lord in the name of Jesus, according to this testimony, please teach me to trust in you more and more each day.

The world teaches us to trust in the news and in the reports of the doctor but in you Oh Lord will I put my trust from day to day.

PRAYER POINTS

1. Father in the name of Jesus, I know you are able to do the impossible so I will trust in you to build me up because you are the God of Luke 1:37

2. I shall overcome all my battles, I shall overcome my enemies, I shall overcome my flesh, I shall overcome poverty, I shall overcome all challenges, I shall overcome the frenemies. I will overcome by the blood of the lamb and by the word of my testimony in Jesus Name!

3. Father in the name of Jesus, I receive the power to trample upon serpents and scorpions and I shall not be affected because I have power and dominion

4. Lord enable me to operate in your power and anointing to live above sin and unrighteousness, lawlessness and backwardness. Build me up Oh God!!! (Pray fervently)

5. I receive power to study the Word of God, work the Word and watch the Word work

for me and I will pray without ceasing in Jesus Name

6. Prophesy over your own life and begin to decree that no one will pull you away from the love of Christ and decree that you will make heaven

Day 8
DELIVER ME

In the book of John Chapter 8, a story is told of a woman who was "caught red handed in the act of adultery" and was led in by the Pharisees and was placed before everyone and Jesus. They then told Jesus that the law states that she must be stoned.

The Pharaohs of this woman's life; these Pharisees were bent on stoning her but failed to drag in the other party in the "act of adultery" - why? Because they were hypocrites. They had selfish interests and motives otherwise they would have judged fairly.

Two had tango'd but she was about to be stoned. I believe that in that moment, the only prayer in that woman's mind was "Lord Jesus DELIVER ME!" Jesus stooped low to write in the dirt (basically gathering the woman's thoughts through the spirit of discernment) and said to the accusers, "let the sinless one, be first to cast a stone!" and he continued to write in the dirt. All of them; from oldest to youngest dropped their stones and left the woman alone.

PRAYER POINTS

1. Father by your mercy! Deliver me today in Jesus Name.

2. I may not have committed adultery and I may not have been caught but deliver me from the ones planning to stone me to death, deliver me from my mind, deliver me from evil.

3. Father by your mercy deliver me from the Pharisees of my life playing God over my situation.

4. Lord Jesus may you rise up and challenge my challengers – Jesus may you say a word to my Pharisees and make them drop the stones they planned to stone me with.

5. Father if there be any deliverance needed in my life (from anything or anyone) may you lead me and deliver me by fire in Jesus name.

6. Place your hand over your head and pray "Lord deliver me, deliver me right now in the name of Jesus Christ" I need your supernatural deliverance right this moment.

7. Deliver me from death, depression, distraction, disaster, diseases, dumbness, divorce, derailment and set me free now and forever in Jesus mighty name!

8. Dear Lord Jesus, please deliver me from the one tormenting my night and day, in real life and in my dreams, deliver me from the spiritual demons and the ones who are in flesh and free me from their torment in Jesus name.

Day 9
CONFUSION CANCELLED

There are days when confusion sets in over a certain decision you have to make or a situation that springs up and suddenly overwhelms your entire being. What do you do on those days? As humans, our thinking faculties kick in to overdrive and you begin to act naturally and forget that we live better as supernatural beings designed and bought by the blood of the lamb. We tend to panic, cry, lament and seek solution from friends and family. Some even isolate themselves completely withdrawn from the world which fosters depression. As children of light, this should NOT be our story.

When confusion sets in, it helps to meditate on scripture and cast your mind back to other times when you have been in this position and begin to reflect on HOW the Lord brought you out of it. It helps to intentionally take out time from what seems like no time to waste and just cast your cares but reflecting on how good God has been to you. During that time of reflection, answers will come and things will supernaturally realign for you. Gratitude to God realigns you back to Him and His promises for you.

One short yet powerful scripture that helped me is in Psalm 71:21 - You will restore me to even greater honor and comfort me once again. When you read something that resonates with your spirit, you begin to stand on that scripture and pray fervently. God sends help and comfort to those who ask!

PRAYER POINTS

1. In Psalm 71:21, David cried that you should restore him to even greater honor and comfort him once again. As you did it for David, may you do it for me also in Jesus name.

2. Lord, I have been here before and wept unto you before, please comfort me once again.

3. The bible says in 2 Corinthians 4:8 "we are pressed on every side by troubles, but we are not crushed. We are perplexed, but not driven to despair." In the name of Jesus, I will not be crushed, I will not be driven to despair, I will stand and God will bring me out of confusion.

4. Oh my soul, why are you downcast, hear the word of the Lord, rise up – take up thy bed and walk. Every bed of affliction risen up against me, I will not lay on you anymore. I am walking in power, in might, in sound mind and in the Light of God.

5. I prophesy clarity over my mind; in the name of Jesus clarity is mine and direction comes now as I begin to walk in Jesus name (walk around and confess this).

6. Everything and every person that brings confusion into my life, I drive you out of my life now by the power in the name of Jesus Christ. Flee from me now for my God is not the author of confusion but of peace according to 1 Corinthians 14:33.

7. Thank you my Father, thank you for wiping my tears, thank you for joy that cometh now, thank you for peace now, thank you for your wisdom that cancels confusion

Day 10
LOCKED UP BUT NOT LOCKED OUT

Peter was locked up in jail. Not everyone will relate to his story because we have never been in jail nor does anyone plan to go to jail but some people have physically been in jail and grateful to be out of jail now, some are still locked up in jail whether innocent or guilty praying to come out soon. The main point to this inspired title is that some who are not in jail are still locked up emotionally, spiritually and in other ways but the point is that we are not locked out of God's will and desires for us.

There are a lot of people who are bound in various ways and like Peter; they are knocking on the door waiting for just one answer to their prayer, waiting for someone to hear them knocking. You will not be locked out in Jesus name.

Acts 12:12-14

When he realized this, he went to the home of Mary, the mother of John Mark, where many were gathered for prayer. He knocked at the door in the gate, and a servant girl named Rhoda came to open it. When she recognized Peter's voice, she was so overjoyed that, instead of opening the door, she ran back inside and told everyone, "Peter is standing at the door!" "You're out of your mind!" they said. When she insisted, they decided, "It must be his angel." Meanwhile, Peter continued knocking. When they finally opened the door and saw him, they were amazed.

PRAYER POINTS

1. Father thank you for the doors that you have opened unto me and my family this year. I thank you for every single door (marital, financial, physical, emotional, institutional, spiritual).

2. In the name of Jesus, I will not be locked up in any marital bondage, I will not be locked up in financial bondage of debt, I will not be locked up in a health challenges or emotional turbulence.

3. As I knock on the great effectual doors to open up unto me, I will not be locked out in Jesus name.

4. There was a delay in opening the door for

Peter because Rhoda was too excited, anyone who is causing a delay in my life, Father speed up the process and open the door yourself in Jesus name.

5. My Father in heaven, give me the grace, strength and ability to be persistent while knocking and cause my breakthrough to manifest in Jesus name.

6. Everything and anyone that stood in my way before, I challenge you with persistence and diligence, you must open up for me in Jesus name.

7. Rhoda insisted that it was Peter at the door, she was sure that it was Peter but they said she was out of her mind. Lord, anyone you have sent to open my door, let them not be confused by nay-sayers and enemies of progress in Jesus name!

8. Thank you Lord for opening my door of success, breakthrough, thank you for not locking me out, thank you for the shouts of joy that will be heard when this door is opened!

Day 11
MIRACLE MONEY

However, we don't want to offend them, so go down to the lake and throw in a line. Open the mouth of the first fish you catch, and you will find a large silver coin. Take it and pay the tax for both of us.
—Matthew 17:27

Jesus did not like owing taxes (bills). If he did not like it, why do we fall short in this area? It is because we do not understand that He is above and not beneath bills. We believe that bills are our Masters so we work to pay bills but on the contrary, Jesus paid his tax bill miraculously. Wouldn't you love to pay every bill or debt you have miraculously? Even as I type this, I am led to take a bill of mine and sometimes they pile up don't they?

I am led to use my bills as an example, I will use multiple bills as an example because I do not want to limit my God. These bills will be paid miraculously tomorrow; not from a paycheck that I am expecting nor from any of my businesses where money is expected tomorrow. If Jesus commanded Peter to go to the lake, cast a line, and open the mouth of the first fish to withdraw a large coin to pay off the debt, the same will happen for you and I and we will not have to catch a fish to pay our bills. Do you have the faith to see this miracle? That is the question!

PRAYER POINTS

1. Thank you Father for life. I am alive to pray about my bills so that is worth thanking you for alone, I thank you for the life of my family because they are not stuck with my debt.

2. In Jesus name, all my bills this month and for the rest of my life will be paid supernaturally under the order of Matthew 17:27 – I declare it so in the name of Jesus.

3. Father, let miracle money locate me and cause all these bills and debts to be wiped off forever.

4. There is nothing impossible for you to do Lord and so I stand in agreement with your word that my bills are never delinquent but paid on time and in full from today in Jesus name.

5. Father, I have my mustard seed faith and my big bills, student loans, etc. – I choose my mustard seed faith and command all my debt erased and nullified just as if they never existed.
   Matthew records this conversation, "You don't have enough faith," Jesus told them. "I tell you the truth, if you had faith even as small as a mustard seed, you could say to this mountain, 'Move from here to there,' and it would move. Nothing would be impossible – Matthew 17:20

6. Father, I command every financial lack to move and never return in Jesus name. I command miracle money to come and I will testify about this in Jesus name!

7. Thank you Father. I know You have done it.

Day 12
INCREASE MY FAITH

Faith is the confidence that what we hope for will actually happen; it gives us assurance about things we cannot see.

—Hebrews 11:1

I love this scripture because it speaks about two words that work together always. Faith and Confidence. You cannot have faith and lack confidence. It is impossible. When people lack confidence, it is called fear and faith mixed with fear is failure. We must be confident to believe that what we hope for will ACTUALLY happen. We prayed about miracle money in the previous lesson and a lot of people will pray the same prayers I prayed yet they will not receive the miracle money. Why? Because they lack the faith.

Some will argue that they don't lack the faith

but they would have uttered a statement in the morning that cancels the prayers and faith they had at night when they prayed. When you are confident, all the words you speak are confident. I will buy my first home in 2018 is not bragging, it is confidence that what I hope for will actually happen and Faith gives us the assurances about things we cannot see.

PRAYER POINTS

1. Father thank you for the faith to believe in You and your sovereignty!

2. You are sovereign and without faith it is impossible to please you, therefore increase my faith oh Lord my God. I want to please you.

3. Father, please guide my mouth that words will not negate what I pray for.

4. I ask in the name of Jesus that my confidence will be stronger in you and because of the word of God in Hebrews 11:1.

5. Everything that I have confidence in will actually happen thus I pray that I will (state your case).

6. Thank you Father for that beautiful BMX X6, thank you for the jaw dropping success in my businesses, thank you for loyal customers and followers, thank you for a global ministry, thank you for a faithful loving husband, thank you for all the wealth and riches in my home, thank you for my amazing children, thank you for the gifts made manifest through me.

7. Thank God for ALL the things you are hoping for and your hopes, dreams, aspirations and plans shall not be dashed in Jesus name!

Day 13
THE HOLY SPIRIT

"There is so much more I want to tell you, but you can't bear it now. When the Spirit of truth comes, he will guide you into all truth. He will not speak on his own but will tell you what he has heard. He will tell you about the future.

—John 16:12-13

This is so powerful! So I don't have to see a psychic or a fortune teller to know what the future holds? No you do not. You do no need to check your horoscope, nor pay a spiritual doctor to tell you what is coming your way. You only need the sweet Holy Spirit. Life without the Holy Spirt is like a water bottle with no water in it when you are thirsty; it is useless.

A Christian without the Holy Spirit is an empty water bottle and the Bible says "of your belly shall flow rivers of living water" – so you

NEED the Holy Spirit to be real and evident in your life. You can distinguish a real Christian from something else by the Holy Spirit. A carrier of the Holy Spirit is identifiable; they are FULL and not EMPTY of the Lord!

PRAYER POINTS

1. Sweet Holy Spirit, you are the difference maker! I want you to come into my heart and make a difference in my life from today.

2. In Micah 3:8 the bible says "but as for me, I am filled with power, with the Spirit of the Lord and with justice and might" therefore I receive the filling of power, I receive the Spirit of God (receive it, pray it and receive it by praying for the infilling of the Holy Ghost with the evidence of speaking in tongues).

3. For those who are tired and depleted and nothing interests you anymore, pray earnestly for the Holy Spirit and pray in tongues until you receive strength (Pray in tongues for 5 minutes non-stop until you sense a shift in your spirit man) Let's Go!

4. Sing some songs of worship, worship now in Spirit for God is looking for those who will worship Him in Spirit and in Truth – tell Him the truth about how you feel and pour your heart out.

5. Fill me up Lord, till I overflow – I need your power, I need your Spirit to move, breathe, work, live, survive and to rule over my flesh, over my desires, over my thoughts.

6. Acts 1:8 speaks of a power that comes upon you when the Holy Spirit comes upon you, so to receive the power you have to receive the Holy Spirit. Begin to thank Him now for that power!

Day 14
I SHALL OVERCOME

Life can be so overwhelming at times and we often find ourselves at our wits end. We have so many challenges, we face so much on a day to day basis and the list is long and exhausting but my Jesus said, "here on earth you will have many trials and sorrows but take heart, because I have overcome the world." (John 16:33)

Jesus overcame the world (the world!) all the things that life has thrown at you, Jesus overcame it all when He died on the cross for you and I. So look at the challenge with your health, your job, business, finances, children, ministry, marriage, your spiritual life, depression, the habits, the family, the friends who stabbed you in the back, the messy divorce, the court cases, the immigration battle, the credit problems, the debt, the lack, the stress, the disappointment, the rejection, the failure, the exams you tried to pass, the college you tried to get into, the one who walked away, the divorce, the long standing battles – look at it all and confess over your life that you shall OVERCOME it just like Jesus did!

PRAYERS POINTS

1. Jesus I thank you for dying for me; you died for my sins and my struggles - you overcame it all so I receive the grace today to overcome.

2. Father wash me with the overcoming blood that was shed on Calvary and help me to overcome all these challenges.

3. Today I give you my battles, I give you all the stress, take it all and give me the overcoming Spirit, give me power to overcome it all in Jesus name.

4. Lead me beside the still waters Oh God and restore my soul, I have been down and out but today I receive total restoration of my body, mind and soul in Jesus name.

5. The battle starts in the mind and finishes in the mind before it is spoken out – Jesus said it was finished after it was settled in His mind. Today, I settle it in my mind that all that I have faced in life is FINISHED – I have overcome in Jesus mighty name!

6. Any power that wants to keep me fighting when Jesus tells me that I have overcome, I command you finished in Jesus name!

7. Anything that contributes to battles in my life, you are a liar, you have failed today because I have received the power to overcome just like Jesus did.

8. Sickness and disease, you shall not prevail over me for I have overcome, I am healthy, I am renewed, I overcome you by the blood of the lamb and in Jesus name.

9. Anything and anyone that wants to limit me this year, hear the word of the Lord – I am an overcomer, nothing can stop me because I belong to Jesus and He overcame!

Day 15
I SHALL NOT BE LUKEWARM

I know your deeds, that you are neither cold nor hot. I wish you were either one or the other! So, because you are lukewarm—neither hot nor cold—I am about to spit you out of my mouth.

—Revelations 3:15

It is amazing that the last book of the Bible is the where this profound statement was made. Have you ever wondered why it was not in the earlier books of the Bible. Why wasn't this told to Adam and Eve, or to David or Solomon? The book of Revelations is the book of reflections and a book that speaks of the visions of the world coming to an end and what the end would be like for many Christians who have heard the word of faith but still choose to live life as they please.

The Bible says in 1 Peter 4:17 for the time is come that judgment must begin at the house of God: and if it first begin at us, what shall the end be of them that obey not the gospel of God?

If judgement is to begin with us in the house of God, is it not time to ponder on the state of the Christian life? Are we lukewarm or are we hot and on fire for God? What will it be like to have lived and walked the Christian walk only for God to tell us that He is about to spit someone out of His mouth. God forbid that it will be you or I. Today let us take a critical look at our Christian walk and make a careful assessment by the leading of the Holy Spirit. Are you hot or cold or neither?

PRAYER POINTS

1. Thank you Lord for your words in the book of Revelations, I will commit to reading the rest of this book to gain divine knowledge.

2. Father, I have not been all that I should be in my walk with you, I am neither hot nor cold (be real with yourself and repent today of lukewarm Spirit if this applies to you, if not, thank God!)

3. I need your help with this topic Lord, how do I become hot for you? I want to know, I want to be connected, I want to be on fire, I want to be active for you but show me how Lord.

4. Father may you connect me today to the source of power so that I can be on fire for you.

5. Lord my spiritual life needs help, connect me to those that will help me in my spiritual walk.

6. Father I commit my whole life before you, may you show me the things that take me away from loving you like I ought to and put me back in line with you.

7. I surrender my life and my will to you Lord and command every coldness in my life to receive fire now, I remove myself from anything that makes me lukewarm and I commit to starting again.

Day 16
I FORGIVE!

And forgive us our sins, as we have forgiven those who sin against us.

—Matthew 6:12

REALLY? Have we really forgiven those who sinned against us or do we just say we have forgiven! Do you know how you can tell that you have forgiven the person you say you have forgiven? You will know that you have forgiven them when you can honestly pray for them. I do not mean the kind of prayer you pray when you want your favorite team to win against the team you do not support. I mean a prayer for them. Many have not reached this level yet but they believe they have forgiven.

True forgiveness is what Jesus did on the cross when He said "Father forgive them for they do not know what they are doing!" Wow! In truth, the ones who hurt you did not know what they were doing. If they only knew that when they hurt you, they were hurting Jesus because you are now IN Christ Jesus. You see, your life (the life they are trying to disgrace and torment) is hidden in Christ Jesus according to Colossians 3:3 "for you died, and your life is now hidden with Christ in God. So it's time to laugh because anyone who touches you, touches God!

PRAYER POINTS

1. Father I want to thank you because you first forgave me and died for me on the cross of Calvary. You died before you even knew me, you practiced advanced forgiveness that day on the cross and for this, I am very grateful.

2. Father please forgive for I have lacked knowledge about forgiveness and I have held so many things and so many people in my heart thinking I forgave but I really did not.

3. Lord Jesus help me today, I want to forgive _____ for how they offended and abused me, I forgive and let go of all

the pain right now in Jesus name.

4. From today, I pray for _____ and I pray that you forgive them for they did not know what they were doing when they did those things to me and said bad things about me. I forgive them for the malicious lies, I forgive the way they took advantage of me and I forgive all those who supported them.

5. Forgive them all. Forgive the cheating spouse, forgive the ex, forgive the friend, the sibling, the parent, the teacher who told you that you would never make it, forgive the liars, forgive the one who won and took it all, forgive that child, forgive that grandparent or family member, forgive the one who stole your innocence, forgive them ALL. They touched God when they touched you. You JUST have to believe that!

6. Father I forgive myself for harboring the pain for this long, I forgive myself for allowing myself to be bound for so long but thank you for opening my eyes.

7. Lord Jesus help me to let go completely and remember it no more in bitterness or pain.

8. I choose to be like you Jesus and rise as you did on the third day – when you rose, it was the greatest sign of forgiveness (He could have remained a ghost and tormented the Pharisees like we would have done; he could have haunted those who beat him and the people who hung him on the cross but He did not; that is our GOD!)

9. Today, I choose forgiveness and freedom from unforgiveness that has locked me in a web of lies all this while. Today I declare that I am free!

10. I gain back my power now – there is power in forgiveness and I want that power now to walk with my head up high knowing that you are proud of me Lord for walking in your image and in your Character! It is well with those who hurt me, I pray for them right now and ask the Lord to have mercy upon them!

Day 17
I CAN DO ALL THINGS!

I can do all this through him who gives me strength.
—Philippians 4:13

I never knew it would be possible to get this book done this year. I have stalled on writing since August for several reasons but all of a sudden the inspiration came and over the past few days I have been writing daily. It is amazing the things that you can accomplish not because you set your mind to do it but because of the One who gives you the strength to do it.

What have you procrastinated for so long? Perhaps going back to school, starting a business, starting a ministry, forming a fellowship, accomplishing a set goal? Whatever it is, if you will realize that it is God that gives the strength and the inspiration to do these things should come from Him and not from any other means, then you will be able to do ALL things!

PRAYER POINTS
- I can do ALL things through Christ who strengthens me!
- I can do ALL things through Christ who strengthens me!
- I can do ALL things through Christ who strengthens me!
- I can do ALL things through Christ who strengthens me!
- I can do ALL things through Christ who strengthens me!
- I can do ALL things through Christ who strengthens me!
- I can do ALL things through Christ who strengthens me!

When I was about to give birth to my first child in September 2006, the Nurse asked me if she could give me epidural and at that moment she awaited a response of yes or no but what she heard surprised her. I simply replied "I can do all things through Christ who strengthens me!" She waited to hear a yes or no but I repeated "I can do all things through Christ who strengthens me!" Within ten minutes, He helped me and I delivered a baby boy!

I prophesy over your life this day that all the things that you could not do on your own; all the things that required a boost, a shot, a drink, a man, or a woman you will begin to do it supernaturally because you can do ALL things through Christ who strengthens you!
I declare over your life that you will DO, you will ACCOMPLISH and you shall BREAKTHROUGH in Jesus Name! I decree that people will ask you HOW DID YOU DO IT? And your response will be "I can do all things through Christ who strengthens me!"

Day 18
I WILL NOT WORRY!

Therefore I tell you, do not worry about your life, what you will eat or drink; or about your body, what you will wear. Is not life more than food, and the body more than clothes? Look at the birds of the air; they do not sow or reap or store away in barns, and yet your heavenly Father feeds them. Are you not much more valuable than they? Can any one of you by worrying add a single hour to your life? —Matthew 6:25-27

What's the use in praying if we will turn around after midnight prayers and worry about our health, our bills, our children, our careers, our future, our marriages, food on the table, roofs over our heads, our haters, our failed relationships, past mistakes or our single life?

PRAYER POINTS
1. Father I want to thank you for my life, for what we eat and drink and how you keep us day after day. Thank you for all you have

done for us Lord, we (you and on behalf of your family) are so grateful. Honor Him!

2. Lord I thank you for the thoughts you have for me are thoughts of good and not evil to bring me to an expected end according to Jeremiah 29:11 – thank you for all the thoughts and how you make them manifest in my life.

3. Father I want to thank you for how to feed the birds of the air and how you count me more valuable than birds, I thank you that you have never let me down nor left me abandoned.

4. Thank you for how you protect me and my family year after year and how you see us through troublesome times; hurricanes, floods, sickness, lack, job loss, financial stress and burdens yet you continue to be good to us always.

5. Father my times are in your hands, I hand over all my worries unto you and ask that you will keep me in perfect peace as I keep my mind fixed on you (Isaiah 26:3)

6. Thank you for taking all my worries and handling them one by one and giving me a new song.

7. Father contend with those things that contend with me and fight against those that fight against me so that I can be free of worry and anxiety.

8. Lord I thank you because I know that you have done it in Jesus Name!

Day 19
I MUST ENDURE

The temptations in your life are no different from what others experience. And God is faithful. He will not allow the temptation to be more than you can stand. When you are tempted, he will show you a way out so that you can endure.

—1 Corinthians 10:13

This is my favorite scripture in all of the Bible and I have read it in so many translations one of which states that NO TRIAL OR TEMPTATION (Nothing you are going through) is different from what others have experienced so why carry it over the top of your head like it is the end of the world? It is NOT the end of the world my friend, get up, dust your shoulders off and keep it moving! YOU MUST ENDURE!

You may have gone through a lot in the previous year and it is inevitable so a lot of things will still happen but if we spend so much time dwelling on one thing refusing to get off the nail we got stuck on in previous years, how will we be able to cope when the next issue arises? The devil is accustomed to throwing nails on the ground but it is the believer's job to identify nails and keep from stepping on them. However when we do find one stuck to our feet, bend down, pull it out, make a joyful noise and keep moving. I don't care if you have to limp all the way to your destination. Limp in style and get to that destination you planned and prove the devil a liar!

PRAYER POINTS

1. The simplest prayer is – Father, HELP ME!

2. Jesus endured so Lord help me to have the same grace that Jesus had while He was alive! The grace to not look like what I have been through, Lord please bless me with it in Jesus name.

3. All my battles, all my struggles, all the hurt and pain I have suffered, I hand them over to the Lord today and I ask for your faithfulness in enduring it all in Jesus name.

4. Everything frustrating my joy and peace in the Lord, I attack you with endurance and strength because I can do all things through Christ who strengthens me.

5. When life feels like a rollercoaster and it has been a series of ups and downs, ask God to step in and take over – Lord take over now, I give the reins of my life over to you, take the wheel and make me whole again.

6. Father in Jesus name, I ask for the overcomer's anointing to overcome any situation that seems too hard for me to bear right now.

7. Father drain out of me every blood that links me to struggles in life and unending battles and give me a the blood transfusion of Jesus so that I can endure and excel in life.

Day 20
SPEAK LIFE

Death and life are in the power of the tongue: and they that love it shall eat the fruit thereof.
—Proverbs 18:21

As we start to round of these 21 days of prayer, I want you to get accustomed to speaking positively into your life, about your life and to anyone you come in contact with.

Death and life are in the power of the tongue so this tells me that the tongue is really the most powerful weapon we have so we must learn to use it wisely.

I remember some things I said this year in annoyance, those things happened and thankfully most of the things I said came to pass and caused me to thank God for the power that He gave unto me. You can drive out sickness, disease, evil spirits, evil people, bad bosses, wicked friends, sexually perverse boyfriends or girlfriends, adulterous spirits and even flies with the power of your tongue.

Yes you can, try it and see but be mindful of the things that you say when happy or when sad because those things you sad actually manifest. When you are feeling down, please be extremely careful of how you describe your feelings because you will only create more of that feeling and the same goes for joy, when you are a joyful person, you create more circumstances of joy!

PRAYER POINTS
1. Father I thank you for the power that lies on my tongue, thank you for blessing me with a mouth to speak.

2. I ask for forgiveness for the things that I have said in the past with my mouth that have caused me to experience the things that I have experienced and I thank you for the great things that I have experienced because of the positive things I have said also.

3. Today I make a covenant with my mouth to only speak positively about my life, concerning my circumstances, concerning my health, my family, my little children and my finances etc.

4. From today Lord help me to keep quiet when I have nothing positive to say and help me to speak up when I ought to speak up.

5. In Luke 1:5:19 Zechariah was a righteous man but when an angel appeared to him to foretell of a powerful son that was to be born unto him, he did not know how to keep from being negative so he said to the angel, "How can I be sure this will happen? I'm an old man now, and my wife is also well along in years." He confessed impossibility. Father, I too have confessed unknowingly some impossibilities, forgive me father and help me to refrain for negative confessions.

6. In verse 19, the angel said, "I am Gabriel! I stand in the very presence of God. It was He who sent me to bring you this good news! But now, since you didn't believe what

I said, you will be silent and unable to speak until the child is born. For my words will certainly be fulfilled at the proper time." Father please forgive me for any blessing I may have driven away because of my mouth, I am sorry and I ask for a fresh tongue sanctified by your blood.

7. Lord Jesus I ask that you purify my mind because my mind is where it all takes place before it proceeds out of my mouth. Please Lord create in my a clean heart and renew a right spirit within me (Psalm 51:10)

8. I release, I repent and I retract every evil pronouncement over _____ and I ask for forgiveness in Jesus name. I ask for the power to do better with my thoughts and with my words from this day forward in Jesus name.

9. I cancel all negative pronouncements ever uttered knowingly or unknowingly and ask for God's mercy not to let the words of my mouth cause negative occurrences, I wash myself with the blood, I sanctify my mind and my mouth today in Jesus name!

10. I declare that I am not a victim, I am a victor. I decree that I am not the tail but the head, I am not average but accomplished, I am not a loser but a landowner, I am not crazy but confident, I am not sad, I am a success in Jesus name. Prophesy over your life now!

Day 21
PROPHESY OVER YOUR LIFE!

I wish you could all speak in tongues, but even more I wish you could all prophesy. For prophecy is greater than speaking in tongues, unless someone interprets what you are saying so that the whole church will be strengthened.

Saints, you are the Prophet over your own life and you have to power to speak into your life. Stop letting people speak into your life, stop giving people so much power to prophesy over you and tell you visions and prophesies, you would do better on your own with the power that God gave you!

Apostle Paul gave us the secret weapon to greatness in this bible verse and you ought to run with it today and for the rest of your life – "you have to prophesy because prophecy is greater than speaking in tongues you can interpret what you say (we ought to pray for this gift too).

I believe that mirrors were not created so that we could check out how handsome or how beautiful we are but so that we could speak into our lives and tell the person in the mirror some things that can take the person from zero to hero. The bible says that David encouraged himself in the Lord; he may have not done so before a mirror but he spoke to himself and this helped him through his challenges in life and caused him to overcome every battle of life and death. You must encourage yourself in the Lord in the Spirit by speaking more in the Spirit and by telling yourself the things you want yourself to experience. Let's go ahead and begin the exercise of prophesy and this should be something you do constantly if you want to see a rapid transformation.

PROPHESY:
1. I am a winner in life and I can do all things through Christ who strengthens me.

2. I am protected by the blood of Jesus which makes me stronger and above sickness and disease.

3. I am the righteousness of God therefore I can and will live above sin.

4. I have the wisdom of God, I can foresee and foretell everything that is around me.

5. I am the voice of God therefore my tongue is anointed and whatever I say begins to happen from the moment I say it. There shall be no delay in the things I say from today onwards.

6. I have the anointing of Elijah and Elisha combined and call fire to fall upon any witchcraft tormenting my life and the life of my loved ones.

7. I banish every spiritual wickedness, spiritual husband or wife tormenting my life or the life of my husband or my children and my family members.

8. Speaking of husband – Kabosh! he is BLESSED, righteous, upright, loyal, loving, humble and loving to the height that Jesus loved the church and gave His life for us.

9. I speak that my husband is my crown and I prophecy that we will serve the Lord together in oneness, He will be my heart

and I will be His and we will make our God proud.

10. I pull down every distraction and every spirit of distraction from my life and I command negative people to go and never return.

11. My ministry is a success and cannot be destroyed because it will reach the nations and nations shall be blessed by me, my husband and my children.

12. The seed of the righteous is delivered and therefore my children are delivered from every spiritual wickedness, they are the head and not the tail and the have the power just like I do to trample over serpents and scorpions and they cannot be harmed.

13. My eyes are sharp to see, my ears are clear to hear, my hands are strong to fight, my legs are able to kick the devil back to hell fire and my back can hold many and nurture them to safety.

14. My life is blessed, money is my servant, I live in the best, I drive the best, I fly in the best, I wear the best, I give the best always and people give unto me willingly without reservation.

15. My money will bless the poor and the poor will become rich because of me; victims will become victors because of me and failures will become financiers of my ministry from today.

16. My businesses are thriving and excelling beyond my imagination. People are waiting in line for my services, products and my expertise!

17. I am the head, I am the best woman and role model, I will live and not die, I will employ many people and many children, buildings and schools will be named after me.

18. My children will go to school debt free, they will marry well, they will LIVE and not die; they will accomplish great things, sickness and disease is far from them and wealth and riches belong in their home and their good deeds will last forever according to Psalm 112:3.

19. My sons and daughters will marry their best friend and the one appointed by God to walk the journey of life with them. They are blessed forever and they will impact their generation.

20. Children are the heritage of the Lord, therefore my children will inherit all the blessings of our father Abraham and be blessed throughout out their lives by my Father, Jehovah Shalom my peace!

21. I love you Lord, you are the one who has given me this power, this ability, this grace, this love for humanity and this strength, I ask for a double portion of the power and grace to do more for your kingdom and I ask for the power to DESTROY wickedness in high places and terrorize the kingdom of the devil. As you have stood by me and taken care of me in 2017, you will make the rest of my life the BEST YEARS OF MY LIFE in Jesus name. I Shout 21 halleluyahs right now to my Father, my King, my Banner, My Shalom, My Protector and My all in all.

TESTIMONIES AFTER TRIALS

"Help me praise the Lord! The embassy has approved my document!" —C.J

"I took my state nursing exam on Monday and passed with distinction." —Anne K.

"I just want to thank God for answered prayers. I prayed for my sister concerning employment during the 100-day fire power prayer. Miraculously, she received 3 job offers in one day. Indeed, He is a way maker!
—Yvette Rowe

"During the designated fasting and prayer, I fell sick. I was miserable! I was not happy because I was consistent with the fasting and prayer. The sickness took so much out of me that the devil began enticing me with food. "Just eat a little" was what I heard. "Stop this fasting until you get better" he said. "Take some medication!" My flesh was weak but I

found strength in my spirit! I resisted the devil. I heard the voice of God which assured me that "by [His] stripes, I was healed!" Instantly, strength came upon me and I began to pray and eject every sickness that was lurking in my body. I received instant healing. Hallelujah!"
—Sister B.

Help me to praise the Lord! My Lord has done it! He has broken protocol for my sake. So, my son was to start school in August. I filled out all the paper work necessary. The school contacted me and informed me that I had to provide a specific document. Oh, my goodness, how will I do it? I did not have what they were asking for. I was a foreigner in the land. Will my son not attend school? I joined 5K5 midnight prayer with fasting. My request, to God, was – Father, please break protocol for me. Do what no man can do. Guess what?! As I was praying, one night, I received an email. The email stated that my son's application has been approved and he can start school. My God! My God! He broke protocol for me! —C. Aj

My marriage has been very rocky for a while. My husband and I never saw eye to eye and

we were constantly arguing. I joined 5K5 midnight prayers and ever since then my story has changed! My husband and I have turned a new leaf. He realized (after being let down by everyone) that I am His number one. At the end of the day, I will always stand by him.
—Anne J.

I just want to thank God for praying through you last night. I had been experiencing burning pain in my knee. With faith, I logged onto 5k5 and began the prayer with the group. Automatically, the burning in my knee disappeared. Even after the prayer I checked my knee again…Gone! All pain gone! Praise God. —Zana

I've been following 5k5 for a few weeks now. A friend introduced me to the group. Ever since I've joined with the fasting, God has been showing up! I lost my government job as a minister back home in Liberia. It was all due to politics. I decided that it was time to relocate back to America. Upon arrival, I began searching for employment. The more I searched, the more I received denial. I kept sending my resume out but it was all in vain. I decided to go back to school and work on

my doctorate. In the process, I was offered a position at the college where I used to teach. What manner of man is Jesus?! Hallelujah.
—L.B

I started the 100 days' prayer with you on the 3rd day. You declared that everyone should have a testimony book and write what they want God to do. I thought in my mind, why not try God. So, I wrote down (with faith) "Thank You God for the fruit of the womb". Fast forward to a couple of weeks later... the glory belongs to God! I did a pregnancy test last Wednesday and the Great Physician operated on my womb! The test was positive! I can't shout enough ooo, help me shout and praise the Lord! —N.B

WOG I want to share my testimony! I received my social security number today, they told me it would take weeks to come but it just came in the mail, I am so happy today!
—Prince Annie Okpon, California

I will like to thank you for being such a blessing to me this year as my mentor, big sis, encourager, and the list goes on.... My life has really changed in terms of how to pray, studying the word of God and understanding what it says. It's one thing to read the word, and another to really understand it. You've been such a great teacher too. You've taught me how to live above my challenges, I can continue until tomorrow. Even though I don't join the prayers every day, I still go back sometimes to watch the replay and it's always been so powerful. Praying that God will bless you abundantly and surprise you in this New Year in Jesus name. The Lord will exceed your expectations - far more than you could ever imagine or guess or request in your wildest dreams! Amen! —D. Ajayi

Sister Seyi, when you visited my home in London, you began to pray and you sprinkled water outside my window and said that if there is any snake in this home, you will see the remnant of it outside your home. Truly, the next day as I was taking my son to school I saw remnants of snake skin on the ground and I remembered your prayer. Thank you for staying with us, so many things happened after you left that were confirmations of the things you said right in my living room! Wow, God is with you. —Blooming Seasons

Good news! You prayed with my family and told us right in our home that in seven days my husband would get a job and that we should get ready for the change. After five years of being unemployed... just a few days after you left London, he was called for an interview and he was asked if he would like to join the training immediately. I thank you so much and I glorify God for this breakthrough!
—A.M.A - London

God bless you WOG for the word this morning. Just can't stop singing this song because of your message from 2 Corinthians 4:8.
—Mary

WOG, I had a dream about you! In the dream, I was lying on my bed and the room was very dark. My husband came in and started making love to me even when I was on my period. It felt so uncomfortable. Then all of a sudden, you shouted at him with authority "what do you think you're doing to her?" When we looked where the sound came from, we saw you seated by the side of the room and you were like the only light in the room because every other place was dark. That was how I woke up. I was so mad with myself. I was like sis Seyi just preached about spirit husband few days ago. Why should I still be having such dream? —Nne E.

Good Morning WOG I am blessed to connect with you yesterday; my little sister always invites me to watch but I always ignore to watch .Yesterday was amazing - all your teaching and message was about me! —Gbenreya

Hallelujah I got my work permit WOG, I thank God for his mercy! —T.J.

Good afternoon WOG, sometime ago when I received my first pay I paid my tithe of £22.40 in your ministry and to my surprise when I received my pay slip this week my manager has redone my timesheet and pay me for 48 hours instead of 42 hours I give all the glory to the almighty and your ministry I started following you since I saw you as a guest on another broadcast because my mum when through the same domestic violence in her marriage. I thank the almighty for connecting me with you. I pray that your anointing will continue to flow. Thank you for your teaching and I

have been following your advice which my husband has now been seeing changes in me.
—Henrietta T.

God bless you sister in The Lord. I have been watching you. I'll love for us to connect in the place of prayer. You are a blessing to this generation. Hoping to hear from you soon.
—Yemisi

Sis Seyi, we prayed against spirit husband yesterday on the prayer line. When I went to bed I had a dream a guy I dated before I got married I saw him in my dream telling me I am too far from him he can't able to meet me. I thank God for my deliverance from spirit husband. Amen. —Libby

I don't know if you remember when I asked for prayers so that I get my sponsorship letter to continue with my studies at the University Of Botswana... By the Grace I got my letter TODAY! Thank you very much! —Pako Derrick S.

Thanks for all your prayers ma, my babies and I go on Facebook every night to jump in prayer with you. Thanks again, may God bless you all the time in Jesus name. —Leruna F.

You are very humble person. My spirit is attract to your teaching and honesty. Pastors/prophets or men/women of God should learn from you. Most of them discourage people from God's word seriously. I am glad to have found you, I called you now my mentor!! God bless you... —Luci Lado

I did it tonight for the first time it is was great! You speak out what I think and say and I have come to realize the purpose tonight! Thank you Jesus. I am like Jonah in the Bible, I was really saying I don't want to know and pray for people! I have been praying to God for years to show me the way and my purpose and I found it! I was afraid and did not know what to say when I talk to people and I was afraid to tell them things that they may not want to hear. But God did lead me to listen to you Seyi and It is all clear! Praise the Lord. As of today I will fulfill my destiny! Stay Blessed.
—Thylda Compaore

Come and see the Lord is good. Come and see

the Lord is good. There is nothing He cannot do. Come and see the Lord is good (dancing emoji). My miracle money has started flowing in oooo. Hallelujah. —Abosede A.

That was a good program mom. I just got the link from a friends post and I have been filled with every inspiration and claimed every prophecy. I am in Cameroon. The time difference to follow up is a problem. Please woman of God keep in touch because I need your God given directions and prayers in my life. I love you live show, I love your theme and truly I see the God given talent in you. —Princess Stephy

Good morning WOG. God bless you for what you're doing for His people may he continue to overflow your cup in every way. Thank you so much for praying over my life this morning I can feel my healing going forth. Hallelujah glory to God. Thank you Jesus. —Louise B.

Mommy right after I drank my water that you blessed for us last night during midnight prayer, I sprinkled it in my entire home like you said. I washed my hands also, but I heard the Holy Spirit say wash your face and decree something over your life, right after I did it felt like something left me. I just landed a Job that I had no intention of applying for. I applied for a hospice position, and I was asked what am I willing accept as an hourly wage. I then said 18 dollars an hour with a little fear. 5 minutes after I left the place, I received a call from the company telling me that they couldn't offer me the position that I applied for because it is below my qualifications but that they have a better position working from Monday to Friday 8am to 5pm. Our God is indeed an excellent God. —Chilli N.P

Good morning Sis Seyi. God bless you mightily with the work you are doing for the Kingdom. I want to testify on my healing. I claim it and believe it's permanent in the mighty name of Jesus Christ. 2017 has tried it's self with regards to my health but God has proven Himself faithful ALWAYS. When we started the worship today, I had my eyes shut and I saw clearly something drop out of a body on the back right side. I took it to signify liberation from attacks like a pest of sorts. So when you mentioned the same thing,

I was like my God. Is this what I saw?? My pain was on my left though. I took up my oil and said Daddy left or right today is for me!! As I lay my hand on my back the peace was wonderful. I said God is it just like this??

As I type the doubt wants to creep in but I refuse to give it a chance to register. I want to encourage you Sis. God is surely working through you. There's so much going on in my life, my husband, my business. I trust my God is still in the business of suddenly. I will still testify! God bless you and have a good night.
—Toyin M.

God bless you. This is the first time of listening to you. A friend of my shared your video. I am richly blessed and also empowered listening to you. I thank God for His Grace upon your life.
—Feyi O.

Praise the Lord! I have three testimonies all concerning my children! God did it. Thank you for your prayers. You are wonderful woman of God. —Damilola A.

Hi my Pastor, God has done it for me again

oooooooooo Goodnews Goodnews Goodnews I passed my test. To God be the Glory for this wonderful New Year gift. And thank you for being there for me. —Koko

WOG Every blessings that you have poured in our lives n are still pouring will be in them. My son has gotten so used to you that and he woke up this morning tell me that he dreamt about you sprinkling water and oil on him. At first I showed him photos on Facebook of other sisters just to see if he really knows what he is talking about but he keeps on saying no not them but the other woman and I eventually showed him your picture and he screamed yes this one. She was the one in my dream. I was shocked. I bless God for your life my darling WOG and sister. —Mary

ARE YOU SAVED?

If you are reading this book and you are not certain about your salvation, it is time to become certain. God loves you and sent his son to die for you and I so that we would be saved and not perish. (John 3:16)

If you have been living in sin and today you want to begin a life with Christ simply read out loud the sinner's prayer that many of us have also confessed before.

Lord Jesus I am sorry for all my sins, I ask you to forgive me today and write my name in the book of life. I confess that Jesus Christ is Lord, I confess that He died and rose on the third day just for me. So I invite you to come into my heart, come in to my life and become the Lord and savior of my soul from this day forward. In Jesus name I pray. Amen.

Saint of God, I beseech you now to take

the next right step and find yourself a bible believing Church where you are taught the word of God and where you can be taught to live according to the scripture. In these end times, many churches are not teaching practical lessons on faith and living the life of faith so be careful where you choose to worship.

Ensure that you have a great leader who is sound in teaching the word of God and who lives the life that Jesus commanded us to live. This will help in molding this new life in Christ and ensure that this new beginning is protected.

I love you with the love of Christ, it is well with you and all that concerns you from this day forward in Jesus name. Know this; the battle does not end just because you gave your life to Christ, in fact sometimes it is even intensified because the devil wants to prove to God that this is just a temporary action on your part. Do you want this to be temporary or permanent? Stay holy and sanctified and you shall prevail against all your battles in Jesus Name!